CONTENTS

SO-AJZ-399

Some words are shown in bold, **like this**. You can find out what they mean by looking in the glossary.

A NARROW ESCAPE

It is fall 1620. A tiny ship battles the waves on the vast Atlantic Ocean. It is crammed with people. They are constantly wet, and many are seasick. The weather is increasingly stormy and treacherous. At times, the wind is so strong that the crew members take in all the sails and simply allow the ship to drift—it is too dangerous to try to sail. On October 1, they are once again being battered by wind and waves when a cry goes up: "Man overboard!" One of the passengers, a man named John Howland, has slipped on the wet deck and fallen over the side. However, as he falls, he grabs a rope trailing in the sea. He holds on for dear life, although he is being half-drowned by the wild waves. As the icy water begins to numb his hands, he feels something grab at his clothes. Howland is hoisted back to safety with a long boat hook.

HOW DO WE KNOW?

After this narrow escape, Howland went on to live for another 50 years—unlike the majority of his fellow passengers. He was one of the Pilgrims, and the little ship was the *Mayflower*. This book tells the story of the Pilgrims—why they ended up crossing the Atlantic on the *Mayflower*, and what happened to them after they finally arrived on the shores of North America. But it also examines *how* we know about this voyage. What are the documents and objects that have allowed historians to piece together events that happened nearly 400 years ago?

HISTORY DETECTIVES:
WHAT IS A PRIMARY SOURCE?

In history, a primary source is one that gives us firsthand information about an event or a particular period in time. Primary sources come in many different forms—they can be "eyewitness" accounts, sketches or paintings, documents such as wills or lists, or, from more recent times, photographs or films.

WHO JOURNEYED ON THE *MAYFLOWER?*

Nicola Barber

Heinemann
LIBRARY

Chicago, Illinois

© 2014 Heinemann Library
an imprint of Capstone Global Library, LLC
Chicago, Illinois

To contact Capstone Global Library, please
call 800-747-4992, or visit our web site
www.capstonepub.com

Edited by Andrew Farrow, Patrick Catel, and
Vaarunika Dharmapala
Designed by Steve Mead
Original illustrations © Capstone Global
Library Ltd 2014
Illustrated by HL Studios
Picture research by Ruth Blair
Originated by Capstone Global Library Ltd
Printed in China

17 16 15 14 13
10 9 8 7 6 5 4 3 2 1

**Library of Congress Cataloging-in-
Publication Data**
Barber, Nicola.
  Who journeyed on the Mayflower? / Nicola
Barber.
      pages cm.—(Primary source detectives)
  Includes bibliographical references and
index.
  ISBN 978-1-4329-9602-4 (hb)—ISBN
978-1-4329-9609-3 (pb) 1. Pilgrims (New
Plymouth Colony)—Juvenile literature. 2.
Mayflower (Ship)—Juvenile literature. 3.
Massachusetts—History—New Plymouth,
1620-1691—Juvenile literature. I. Title.

  F68.B25 2014
  974.4'02—dc23   2013015844

Acknowledgments
We would like to thank the following for
permission to reproduce photographs:
Alamy pp. 5, 21 & 56 (© North Wind Picture
Archives), 7 (© Justin Kase z08z), 25 (© Old
Paper Studios), 26 (© David Lyons), 34 (©
Lebrecht Music and Arts Photo Library),
50 (© Universal Images Group [Lake
County Discovery Museum]); Corbis pp.
23 (© Brooklyn Museum), 29 (© Burstein
Collection), 32 & 41 (© Bettmann), 54 (©
PoodlesRock); Courtesy of Pilgrim Hall
Museum p. 11, 30, 36 & 43; Getty Images
pp. 6 (British Library/Robana), 13 (National
Geographic), 15 (Universal Images Group),
16 (Time & Life Pictures), 46 (Boston
Globe), 47 (Kean Collection), 49 (MPI), 53
(Claver Carroll); Library of Congress p. 10;
Shutterstock p. 22 (© Tischenko Irina).

Cover photograph of the Mayflower
Compact, 1620 (engraving, 1859, after
Tompkins Harrison Matteson), reproduced
with permission of Topfoto (The Granger
Collection).

⚠ This is an artist's impression of the *Mayflower* at sea. No pictures of the ship exist, so historians and artists rely on descriptions from primary sources.

MEET WILLIAM BRADFORD

The account of Howland's near-drowning is found in a journal entitled *Of Plymouth Plantation* by one of the Pilgrim leaders, William Bradford. We will find out a lot more about Bradford and about his history of the Pilgrims throughout this book. The document is a primary source that gives us important information about what happened to the Pilgrims. Below is a brief extract from Bradford's description of Howland's adventure. To make it easier to understand, some spellings have been changed from the original. For example, *shipe* has been changed to "ship," and *yonge* to "young":

> *In a mighty storm, a lusty young man (called John Howland)…was, with a heel of the ship thrown into [the] sea; but it pleased God that he caught hold of the top-sail halliards [ropes], which hung over board… He held his hold…and then with a boat hook and other means got into the ship again, and his life saved…*

WHAT WAS THE MAYFLOWER?

Where did the ship come from that carried the Pilgrims across the Atlantic Ocean? In the 16th and 17th centuries, *Mayflower* was a very common name for ships—in fact, at that time, there were *Mayflowers* sailing out of almost every port in England, Ireland, and Scotland. It took some detective work in the early 1900s by a naval historian named R. G. Marsden to uncover which of the many *Mayflowers* was the correct one.

▲ The home of Christopher Jones, master of the *Mayflower*, still stands in the town of Harwich, on England's east coast.

TO THE ARCHIVES

There are a few clues from primary sources such as William Bradford's journal about the size and the layout of the ship. Bradford also tells us that the ship's **master** was named Mr. Jones, but he does not give his first name. Marsden went to the **archives** of the High Court of Admiralty in London, the English court that has dealt with disputes and **lawsuits** about ships and cargoes since the 1300s. He reduced the number of possible *Mayflowers* that could have set sail across the Atlantic in fall 1620 to a handful, and then to just one. This *Mayflower* was partly owned by its master, Christopher Jones, and it originally came from Harwich, England.

▲ From 1611, the *Mayflower* was based in Rotherhithe, in London, England. This picture of the commercial docks at Rotherhithe dates from 1813.

HERRING TROUBLES

We know from records kept at busy ports that before the *Mayflower* carried its human cargo across the Atlantic, its job was to carry all sorts of other goods around Europe. In 1609, the *Mayflower* was on the return leg of a voyage to Norway, packed with tar, pine planks, and herring. The ship ran into a storm and had to dump a large part of its cargo overboard to lighten its load. A lawsuit followed, recorded in the High Court of Admiralty, because the *Mayflower* did not deliver the full amount of herring.

In 1620, the *Mayflower* was hired to take a group of **colonists**—the Pilgrims—to North America. This was the ship's and its master's first transatlantic voyage, as well as the first for most (but not all) of the crew.

HISTORY DETECTIVES: PORT BOOKS

We know about the movements of the *Mayflower* before its journey across the Atlantic from records, now held in the National Archives of the United Kingdom, called port books. Merchants importing goods from overseas were required to pay duties (taxes) at the port of unloading. From 1565 until 1799, all of these taxable cargoes were recorded in the port books. About 20,000 survive today. You can find out more about port books at: www.nationalarchives.gov.uk/records/research-guides/port-books.htm.

WHAT DO WE KNOW ABOUT THE *MAYFLOWER?*

The *Mayflower* was about 100 feet (30 meters) long and 25 feet (7.6 meters) across at its widest point. It was modeled on a type of Dutch trading ship called a *fluyt* (pronounced "flight"), with space for cargo below decks. We know from William Bradford's account that it had a capacity of "180 tons"—this means that it could fit at least 180 barrels of wine in its hold. *Fluyts* were built to sail easily at sea with only a small crew. They were, however, not designed to take cargoes of human passengers.

LIVING CONDITIONS

The *Mayflower* had a tween, or gun deck, between the upper deck and its cargo hold. The tween carried cannon and guns for defense. This cramped space was where the Pilgrim passengers lived during the voyage. There were no cabins, no bathroom facilities, and there was nowhere to cook and eat. The height of the gun deck has been estimated at about 5 feet, 6 inches (1.6 meters), so tall people were not able to stand up straight.

The passengers put up makeshift wooden partitions to give families privacy. They used buckets for toilets and for vomiting when seasickness struck— which was frequent in the stormy Atlantic seas. The foul-smelling air can only be imagined, even though the Pilgrims made every effort to scrub their living quarters and air their bedding. For the sake of their health, they went on deck whenever they could, frequently getting in the way of the crew, many of whom grew increasingly irritated with their passengers.

GOD'S PROVIDENCE

William Bradford tells of a sailor who was hostile to the Pilgrims: "He would always be condemning the poor people in their sickness... If he were by any gently reproved, he would curse and swear most bitterly." Bradford goes on to relate how this sailor was punished for his behavior: "But it pleased God...to smite this young man with a grevious disease, of which he dyed in a desperate manner, and so was himself the first that was thrown overboard." For Bradford, this was evidence of the "just hand of God" helping the Pilgrims in their time of need.

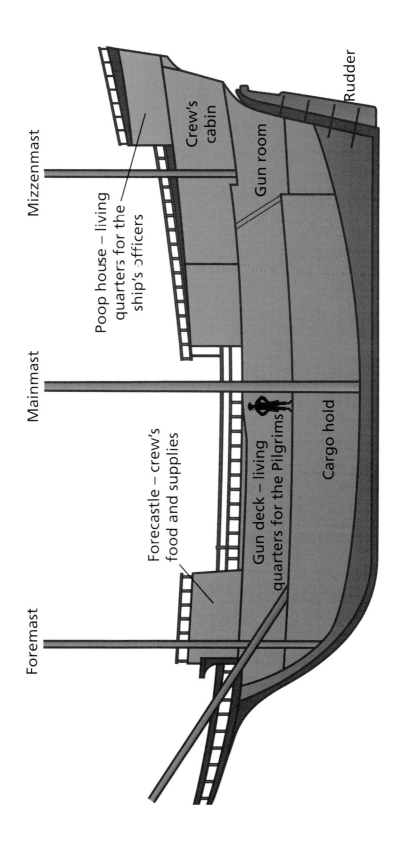

Foremast

Mainmast

Mizzenmast

Poop house – living quarters for the ship's officers

Forecastle – crew's food and supplies

Gun deck – living quarters for the Pilgrims

Crew's cabin

Gun room

Cargo hold

Rudder

△ This diagram of the *Mayflower* shows the main areas of the ship. It is based on accounts of the ship itself and on other similar ships of the time.

9

WHAT DID THEY TAKE?

The cargo hold beneath the gun deck was packed full of the Pilgrims' belongings and provisions. There is no actual list of the things taken by the Pilgrims to North America. But it is possible to look at other primary sources from the period to get a good idea of what they might have needed, including items such as food and drink, clothes, bedding, household objects, tools, and guns. The Pilgrims would have gotten some information about the land they were going to from publications by people who had already been to North America. The best known of these people was Captain John Smith, an adventurer and soldier who made several voyages across the Atlantic. He published books such as *A Description of New England* (1616) to inform and encourage possible settlers.

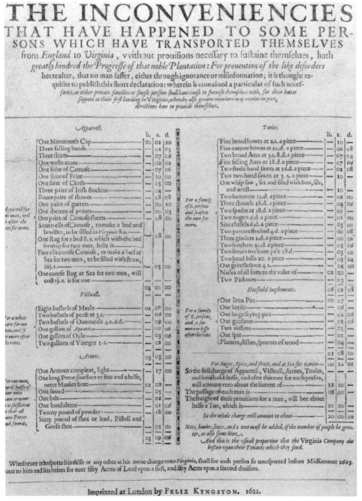

This document from 1622 sets out what a well-equipped colonist should pack for a new life in North America. Many people arrived without the necessary food, clothing, and other supplies to survive.

HISTORY DETECTIVES:
OBJECTS FROM THE MAYFLOWER

Some of the surviving objects that traveled on the *Mayflower* are housed in the Pilgrim Hall Museum in Plymouth, Massachusetts. They include the Brewster chest, which belonged to one of the Pilgrim leaders, William Brewster. A chest was one of the most useful pieces of furniture for a colonist to own—not only could precious belongings be stored inside it, but the chest itself could also be used on the voyage as a makeshift seat, table, or even a bed. The Pilgrims also brought weapons: swords, guns, and ammunition. These were necessary for hunting animals for food, and for defense against possibly hostile **native peoples**. The iron cooking pot below is believed to have traveled on the *Mayflower* with Captain Myles Standish.

You can find out more about the museum and its collections at: www.pilgrimhallmuseum.org.

RECONSTRUCTING THE *MAYFLOWER*

There is no actual picture of the *Mayflower*, although many artists have imagined and reconstructed what the ship looked like based on the historical evidence. In 1955, work began on a life-size reconstruction of the *Mayflower* at a shipbuilding company in Brixham, England. The reconstruction was based on a design drawn up by an American **maritime** architect and historian named William A. Baker, who was an authority on colonial ships. The same materials were used for the reconstruction as would have been found on the original ship—solid oak timbers for the hull, heavy **canvas** sails, tar-covered ropes, and **rigging**.

WHOSE IDEA?

The reconstruction, called *Mayflower II*, was the idea of English businessman Warwick Charlton. During World War II (1939–1945), he had served with U.S. forces. He wanted to celebrate the cooperation between the United States and United Kingdom during the war. He came up with the idea of building a reproduction of the *Mayflower* as a gift for the American people.

MODERN-DAY VOYAGE

In 1957, the reconstruction, *Mayflower II*, crossed the Atlantic Ocean. The crossing took 55 days. The modern-day pilgrims had better living conditions and food than their 17th-century predecessors, although the cabins were stuffy and noisy. Mike Ford, in his book *54 Days Before the Mast*, spoke of his time on board:

> The bunks were in tiny two-man cubicles made of plywood walls...
> Each cabin had one small electric light to be used only when the
> occupant was dressing to go on duty... There were no portholes
> or other ventilation, which meant the vessel had a distinctive
> atmosphere below decks after a few days at sea.

Every Sunday, the crew members dressed in 17th-century costumes and held a service on deck, in memory of the Pilgrims. But what astounded many in the crew was the size of the ship for the number of passengers it carried in 1620. The historian Nathaniel Philbrick later wrote: "Like most people, I was immediately struck by how small the ship seemed... How could 102 people, including three pregnant mothers, have survived more than ten weeks in a space this size?"

WHAT HAPPENED TO THE ORIGINAL MAYFLOWER?

The *Mayflower* returned to England in 1621 and resumed its short journeys between London and France. Master Christopher Jones died in 1622, and the last official record of the ship was made in 1624, when it was declared to be "in ruins." That is all we know for certain, although some people have claimed that the timbers of the *Mayflower* were used to build a barn in the village of Jordans, England.

The captain waves from the stern (back) cabin of the *Mayflower II* as it sails across the Atlantic Ocean. ▷

WHY DID THEY GO?

We know how the Pilgrims crossed the Atlantic, but *why* did they go? What drove this group of people to leave behind their homes and loved ones to venture out on such a dangerous journey? To answer this question, we need to go back briefly to the events of the previous century, when King Henry VIII was the leader of England.

TURBULENT TIMES

Henry broke away from the **Roman Catholic Church** and established an independent Church of England in 1534. His son Edward VI (reigned 1547–1553) introduced **Protestant** forms of worship, including the *Book of Common Prayer*, which laid out the structures and the words of services in the Church of England. However, when Edward died, Henry's eldest daughter, the Catholic Mary I (reigned 1553–1558), reintroduced Catholic practices. Many people were executed or burned at the stake during her reign for refusing to give up their Protestant faith. Elizabeth I (reigned 1558–1603) reinstated the independence of the Church of England from the Roman Catholic Church and reestablished Protestant services held according to the *Book of Common Prayer*.

PURITANS AND SEPARATISTS

Many did not agree with Elizabeth's religious policies. For some people, the reforms of the Church of England did not go far enough. Some Protestants wanted to remove what they saw as "Catholic" practices that remained in the Church of England, such as wearing vestments (special clothes) for services or the **hierarchical** organization of the church from archbishops down to priests. These reformers were labeled **Puritans** because they insisted on "purity" of belief and practice. Other groups of reformers had given up trying to change the church from within and instead gathered in separate congregations to worship. They were known as **Separatists**. To belong to a Separatist congregation, as William Bradford did, was against the law. Bradford starts his journal in 1606 with accounts of the persecution and imprisonment of Separatists by the government and by the church authorities.

▲ Thomas Cranmer, archbishop of Canterbury, is burned at the stake in 1556. During the reign of Queen Mary I, Cranmer was one of the many people who died because they refused to give up their Protestant faith.

REFORMERS VS. THE CHURCH OF ENGLAND

This is how William Bradford described the two sides of the argument, between those who wanted more reform and the church authorities. The **bias** of his writing is clear—the reformers have the "right worship of God," while the Church of England is accused of "lordly and tyrannous power":

> *The one side [the reformers] laboured to have the right worship of God and discipline of Christ established in the church, according to the simplicity of the gospel... The other party [the Church of England], though under many colours and pretences, endeavoured to have the episcopal dignity [dignity of the bishops]...with their large power and jurisdiction [authority] still retained; with all those courts...[and] ceremonies...[as] enabled them with lordly and tyrannous power to persecute the poor servants of God.*

THE SCROOBY CONGREGATION

As a young man, William Bradford became part of a Separatist congregation that was based in Scrooby, England. The congregation met in the home of William Brewster. It was this Separatist congregation that was to form the nucleus of the *Mayflower* Pilgrims. In 1607, several Scrooby Separatists were arrested and imprisoned. With the threat of fines, imprisonment, and, at worst, hanging, the Separatists decided to leave England and move to a place where they would be able to worship without persecution. This place was the Netherlands (Holland).

FREEDOM TO WORSHIP

Since 1579, when the Union of Utrecht had guaranteed freedom in the choice of personal religion, the Netherlands had seen an influx of religious refugees. The Scrooby Separatists were by no means the first people to make the journey across the English Channel. As Bradford wrote of the Pilgrims: "Seeing…that there was no hope of their continuance [in England], by a joint consent they resolved to go into the Low-Countries [the Netherlands], where they heard was freedom of Religion for all men."

▽ Scrooby Manor was William Brewster's house. He held Separatist meetings there in 1606 and 1607.

ESCAPE

Having made the decision to leave, the Separatists made their first attempt to escape England in 1607. Even this was fraught with danger and difficulty, as people were not allowed to travel overseas without permits. The Separatists rented a ship to take them secretly, but they were betrayed by the ship's master. Everyone in the group was arrested and imprisoned, including William Brewster. A second attempt in 1608 resulted in the men escaping to sea, but leaving behind the women and children, who were once again arrested. But, as Bradford recounts, the authorities did not quite know what to do with these troublesome prisoners, and after being "turmoiled a good while," they were allowed to leave England to join their husbands.

WHO IN HISTORY

WILLIAM BREWSTER
ABOUT **1566–1644**
BORN: Scrooby, England

ROLE: **Elder** of the Pilgrim Separatist congregation. Brewster attended England's Cambridge University and worked briefly as a diplomat before returning home to Scrooby. He moved to the Netherlands with the Separatist congregation and worked in Leiden, in the Netherlands, as a tutor and printer. With his wife, Mary, and two of his children, he went to North America on the *Mayflower* and became the religious leader of the new **colony**.

Did You Know?

William Brewster's home, Scrooby Manor, was an impressive house that belonged to the archbishop of York. King Henry VIII stayed there once, and both Elizabeth I and James I liked the "palace" so much that they attempted (unsuccessfully) to buy it. Part of the house still stands today. You can find out more at: www.pilgrimfathersorigins.org/Pilgrim_Fathers_Origins_Tour_Scrooby_Manor.html.

WHAT DID THEY DO?

In the Netherlands, the Pilgrims eventually established a community in the university city of Leiden. For many of the Pilgrims, life in this Dutch city was completely different from what they had known in England. As Bradford tells us in his journal, many of them "had only been used to a plain country life, and the innocent trade of husbandry [farming]." They found themselves in a crowded, cosmopolitan city where they needed to make a living. Around half of the Pilgrims found work in Leiden's thriving cloth industry, while others took up such trades as watchmakers, hatmakers, and merchants.

THE PILGRIM PRESS

William Brewster found life difficult in Leiden. As a gentleman, he was not used to hard manual labor. In order to support his family, he worked as a tutor, and then, toward the end of the Pilgrims' time in Leiden, he set up a printing press. Some of the books he printed were critical of King James I of England, and in 1619, Brewster was forced to go into hiding. He managed to elude capture, slip on to the *Mayflower*, and was next heard of in North America.

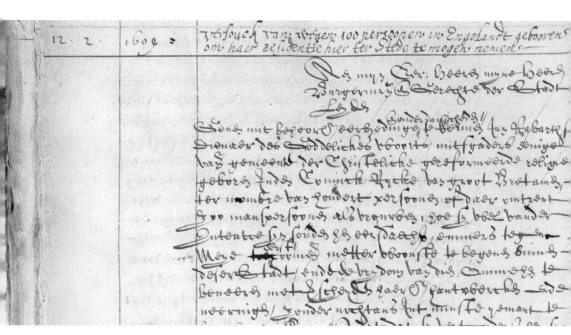

⚠ This is the document, dated February 12, 1609, that gave permission for Reverend John Robinson and about 100 of his fellow Separatists to settle in Leiden in May of that year. The document is part of the Pilgrim Collection held in the Leiden Archives in the Netherlands.

WHY DID THEY DECIDE TO LEAVE?

After 10 years in Leiden, the Pilgrims once again began to consider moving. Bradford gives us several reasons for this:

- The difficulties of earning a living resulted in real hardship and poverty for many of the Pilgrims.
- There were concerns about lack of education for the Pilgrims' children.
- The Pilgrims were also worried that their children were losing their English identity.
- The Pilgrims did not approve of the fact that many people in the Netherlands treated the Sabbath (Sunday) as an ordinary day of the week.
- The political situation was changing, with the threat of war and invasion by Spanish (Catholic) troops.

The Pilgrims could not return to England, so the choice of where to go was quickly narrowed down to North America or Guiana in South America, which had been explored by Englishman Walter Raleigh in the 1590s. Bradford writes of the discussions that took place before a decision was made to go to Virginia. This was the North American colony first settled by the English in 1607, with the establishment of Jamestown. The Pilgrims now had to apply to the Virginia Company for permission to start a new settlement. And since this was an English colony, they needed royal permission to worship freely in their proposed new home. Although they did not get this permission, they were given a royal promise that they would not be "molested [bothered]" if they lived "peaceably" in North America.

WHO TRAVELED ON THE *MAYFLOWER?*

There were 102 Pilgrims on board the *Mayflower* when it left Plymouth Harbor, in England, on September 6, 1620. We know exactly who made the perilous journey because William Bradford listed them in his journal, grouping them into families (see page 22). Bradford's journal is one of the most complete primary sources we have concerning the Pilgrims. As we have already seen, he began it long before the voyage of the *Mayflower*, and he continued it until 1650, by which time the colony was well established. Bradford never intended to publish the journal—it was a historical document written for his family. But the fact that this precious manuscript survived at all is extraordinary.

OLD AND NEW STYLE DATES

The dates used by William Bradford in his journal are Old Style (OS) from the Julian calendar. The Julian calendar was named after the ancient Roman general Julius Caesar. It was in use throughout much of Europe until Pope Gregory XIII introduced a new system, the Gregorian calendar, in 1582. In England and its colonies, both calendars were used between 1582 and 1752, when the New Style (NS) Gregorian calendar became law. At the time the Pilgrims were settling in North America, the two calendars were 10 days apart. This explains why in some sources you may find, for example, the date that the *Mayflower* left Plymouth in England given as either September 6 (OS) or September 16 (NS).

THE STORY OF THE JOURNAL

To start with, Bradford's journal was passed down the generations of his family. Along the way, it was borrowed by several historians, eager to use it to research their own books. It even miraculously survived a house fire. Then, during the Revolutionary War (1775–1783), it disappeared. It is likely that it was taken by British troops, because it next turned up in the bishop of London's library in 1855. Now a tug-of-war started between the British and Americans, both claiming this important manuscript as their own. It was not until 1897 that it was finally taken back to the United States—and a huge banquet was given to celebrate the occasion! Today, Bradford's journal is kept in the Massachusetts State Library.

HISTORY DETECTIVES: A POINT OF VIEW

William Bradford's journal (see right for a woodcut reproduction) is a significant resource for information about the lives of the Pilgrims. However, it is important to remember that it is written from his point of view. It does not necessarily give you a balanced view of the Pilgrims' situation. This does not mean that you shouldn't use it as a primary source—every document is biased in some way. It does mean that you need to read his words carefully; turn to page 39 for a list of questions that help you to do this.

MAYFLOWER PASSENGER LIST

This is the full list of passengers who traveled on the *Mayflower*. William Bradford recorded them in family groups, with children and servants, as shown here. The Pilgrims who died during the first, grim winter of 1620–1621 are marked with an asterisk (*).

John Carver, Katherine his wife
Desire Minter in the care of the Carver family
John Howland, Roger Wilder* two menservants
William Latham servant/apprentice
Jasper More* child in the Carvers' care
William Brewster, Mary his wife
Love and Wrestling their two sons
Richard and Mary More* children in the Brewsters' care
Edward Winslow, Elizabeth* his wife
George Soule and Elias Story* two menservants
Ellen More* child in the Winslows' care
William Bradford, Dorothy* his wife
Isaac Allerton, Mary* his wife
Bartholomew, Remember, and Mary their three children
John Hooke* a servant boy
Samuel Fuller
John Crackston and his son John Crackston
Captain Myles Standish, Rose* his wife
Christopher Martin*, Mary* his wife
Solomon Prower* his stepson
John Langmore* a servant
William Mullins*, Alice* his wife
Joseph* and Priscilla their two children
Robert Carter* a servant
William White*, Susanna his wife
two sons Resolved, and Peregrine born on board the Mayflower
William Holbeck* and Edward Thompson* two servants
Stephen Hopkins, Elizabeth his wife
four children Giles, Constance, Damaris, and Oceanus born at sea

Edward Doty and Edward Leister two servants
Richard Warren
John Billington, Eleanor his wife
John and Francis two sons
Edward Tilley*, Agnes* his wife
Henry Samson and Humility Cooper two children that were their neice and nephew
John Tilley*, Joan* his wife
Elizabeth their daughter
Francis Cooke and his son John
Thomas Rogers* and his son Joseph
Thomas Tinker* and his wife* and son*
John Rigsdale*, Alice* his wife
James Chilton*, his wife
Mary their daughter
Edward Fuller* and his wife*
Samuel their son
John Turner* and two sons*
Francis Eaton, Sarah* his wife
Samuel their son
Moses Fletcher*, John Goodman*, Thomas Williams*, Degory Priest*, Edmund Margesson*, Peter Browne, Richard Britteridge*, Richard Clarke*, Richard Gardiner, Gilbert Winslow
John Alden hired as a cooper at Southampton
John Allerton* and Thomas English* both hired
William Trevore and Richard Ely two seamen hired to stay a year in Plymouth Plantation

⚠ This famous painting, entitled *Embarkation of the Pilgrims*, is by 19th-century American artist Robert Walter Weir. It shows the Pilgrims leaving the Netherlands on board the *Speedwell* (see page 36), ready to join up with the *Mayflower* in Southampton, England.

WHO IN HISTORY

WILLIAM BRADFORD
1590–1657

BORN: Austerfield, England

ROLE: Bradford was the leader of the settlers at Plymouth Colony in Massachusetts and governor of the colony five times between 1621 and 1657. Bradford came from a small farming community near Scrooby, England. When he was about 12, Bradford first attended a Puritan service at a local church. He soon became a member of the Separatist congregation at William Brewster's home in Scrooby. In 1609, he joined the Separatists as they fled to the Netherlands. Ten years later, Bradford played a large part in planning the voyage to North America. He was elected as the second governor of the colony after John Carver died in April 1621.

Did You Know?

When William Bradford left the Netherlands with his first wife, Dorothy, they left behind their four-year-old son, John. It was the last time the boy was to see his mother. Only a few weeks after arriving off the coast of Cape Cod, Dorothy drowned after falling overboard from the *Mayflower*.

WHO WERE THE OTHER LEADERS?

One of the hardest decisions for the Pilgrims was who should go on the voyage across the Atlantic. The religious leader of the group, Reverend John Robinson, stayed in Leiden to care for the congregation that was left behind there. In fact, he died (in 1625) before he was able to make the journey to North America. The next most senior member of the Leiden congregation was William Brewster. He was a church elder—not **ordained** like Reverend Robinson, but responsible for the management of the congregation in Leiden. Brewster agreed to go on the *Mayflower* as the travelers' religious guide, and he became the elder for the new colony.

EDWARD WINSLOW

Apart from William Bradford, the other most important leader of the Pilgrims was Edward Winslow. From a wealthy family, Winslow became involved with the Separatists as a young man when he was traveling in northern Europe. He married Elizabeth Barker in Leiden in 1618 and probably worked with William Brewster in the printing press (see page 18). Elizabeth died during the first winter in Plymouth Colony, but Winslow married the recently widowed Susanna White in 1621—the first wedding in the new colony.

Winslow was a well-educated man of the world, and his standing in the colony quickly grew. He proved to be a skilled negotiator in talks with the local American Indians. He was elected governor of the colony three times. He was also a good writer, and together with William Bradford, he produced a detailed account of the Pilgrims' first year after making landfall. Unlike Bradford's private journal, this manuscript was intended for publication. It was taken back to London by Robert Cushman (see page 33) in 1622 and published in the same year. Its title was *A Relation or Journal...of the English Plantation Settled at Plymouth*, but it became known as *Mourt's Relation* after George Morton (sometimes known as George Mourt), who arranged its publication in England.

◁ This engraving is taken from a portrait of Edward Winslow. It is the only known authentic portrait of one of the *Mayflower* passengers. The fact that Winslow had his portrait painted reflects his status and social standing.

Think About This

Promoting the colony

Although Winslow recounts the difficulties of the Pilgrims' first winter in Plymouth Colony in *Mourt's Relation*, he is also careful to present a glowing picture of the land itself. He frequently skips over the harsher details of hardships and deaths in favor of descriptions of an abundance of trees, animals, and fish for example· "This bay is a most hopeful place, innumerable store of fowl, and excellent good, and cannot but be of fish in their season: skate, cod, turbot, and herring, we have tasted of, abundance of mussels the greatest and best that ever we saw." Why do you think he was so eager to send a positive message about the colony back to England?

WOMEN AND CHILDREN

Because Bradford listed the passengers in family groups, we know that there were 29 women and girls on board when the *Mayflower* sailed in 1620. Many of the Pilgrims worried about whether the "weak bodies" of women would be able to withstand the voyage and the tough conditions afterward. Some chose to leave their wives and children behind, with the intention that they would follow later.

▽ These women are reenacting the lives of the Pilgrims in a re-creation of the small community built by the Pilgrims along the shore of Plymouth Harbor in Massachusetts.

FIRST WINTER

In fact, all the women and girls survived the voyage itself. The *Mayflower* arrived off Cape Cod on November 11, 1620. There then followed many weeks when the men were desperately searching for a suitable site to establish the new colony. Meanwhile, the women and children were forced to stay in the damp, crowded quarters of the *Mayflower*, as it was too dangerous and cold for them to set up camp on shore. In such conditions, it is no surprise that infection and disease spread rapidly. Only five of the eleven women survived to the end of the first winter. One of those survivors, Katherine Carver, died in the spring, only a few weeks after her husband, John. The four remaining women were Eleanor Billington, Elizabeth Hopkins, Mary Brewster (wife of William), and Susanna Winslow.

Think About This

Would you take your children into the unknown?
What would you have done? Risk your children on a perilous sea voyage to an unknown destination? Or be parted from them for years, possibly forever? The Pilgrims had very little information on which to base these difficult decisions. It is interesting that the only Pilgrim who had firsthand knowledge of North America, Stephen Hopkins, chose to take all of his family with him.

DIFFICULT DECISIONS

Many of the Pilgrims made the difficult decision to leave their daughters behind in the Netherlands or England and then send for them once the colony was established. For example, the Brewsters took their two sons with them on the *Mayflower*, but they left behind their daughters, Patience and Fear. The two girls eventually joined their family in 1623. The oldest girl to sail on the *Mayflower* was Priscilla Mullins, who traveled with her brother and parents. All of her family died during the first winter. In fact, many of the children were orphans by the end of that terrible winter.

One Pilgrim who took all of his family with him was Stephen Hopkins. He was the only Pilgrim to have been to North America before, in 1609. Despite shipwreck and many adventures, he was determined to return. He took with him his pregnant wife, Elizabeth, and his children, Constance, Giles, and Damaris. Elizabeth gave birth to a boy, named Oceanus, while at sea. The family was lucky to survive the first winter in the colony, and Stephen and Elizabeth had five more children in the coming years.

WHO WERE THE MEMBERS OF THE CREW?

The first member of the crew to be hired by the Pilgrims as they began to plan their voyage was John Clarke, the ship's **pilot** and mate. The pilot of a ship is responsible for navigation, particularly when the ship is close to land and potential hazards such as rocks and sandbanks. The Pilgrims were eager to hire Clarke because he had previous experience sailing to North America. In 1610, he was pilot on a ship that sailed to Jamestown, Virginia, and in 1619, he sailed once again for North America with a cargo of cattle. The Pilgrims hired him soon after his return from this voyage.

SICK CREW

According to Bradford's journal, while the Pilgrims took care of their sick and dying, the crew did not behave so well to their fellow shipmates:

They that before had been boone [good] companions in drinking and jollity in the time of their health and welfare, began now to desert one another in this calamity, saying they would not hazard their lives for them, they should be infected by coming to help them in their cabins, and so, after they came to die by it, would do little or nothing for them, but if they died let them die...

Master Christopher Jones part-owned the *Mayflower*. He lived in Rotherhithe, in London, England. His intention when he was hired by the Pilgrims was to take them to their settlement site in North America, then sail immediately back to England. But the *Mayflower* arrived later than planned off Cape Cod, and it took the Pilgrims many weeks to find a suitable site. By that time, the same diseases that were affecting the passengers had spread to the crew. Jones realized that he would have to wait until his crew had recovered sufficiently and the weather improved to manage the return voyage. He set sail for England in April 1621, having lost at least 12 crew members, including his gunner, three quartermasters, and the cook.

▲ The *Mayflower* is tossed by wind and waves in the Atlantic Ocean in this imagined scene by Gilbert Margeson.

OTHER CREW JOBS

There were probably around 30 crew members in total on the *Mayflower*. We know some names and their occupations from references in Bradford's journal or other records such as wills.

- Master's mate Robert Coppin: Like Clarke, Coppin also had experience sailing the Atlantic Ocean and had visited Cape Cod before.

- Cooper (barrel-maker) John Alden: All the food and drink on board the *Mayflower* was stored in wooden barrels, so making and repairing barrels was an important job.

- Surgeon Giles Heale: We know his name because he signed the will of William Mullins. He had only just qualified as a **barber-surgeon**, so this was possibly his first job.

Other jobs included carpenter, cook, gunner, boatswains (in charge of the rigging and sails), quartermasters (in charge of the cargo and provisions), and ordinary sailors.

WHAT KIND OF PEOPLE WERE THEY?

At the core of the Pilgrims was the group of Separatists from Leiden led by Elder Brewster. What were the beliefs that bound the Separatists together and led them to make the decision to leave for North America?

TRUE BELIEVERS

The Separatists looked to the Bible as their guide for faith and practice. They rejected the traditions and rituals of the Church of England—for example, they did not use the *Book of Common Prayer* (see page 14), which laid down the words to be used in Church of England services, because they thought prayer should be spontaneous. John Smyth, leader of the first Separatist congregation in Gainsborough, England, said prayer should be "conceived"—created by each individual to express his or her own faith. Similarly, Separatists thought that their church should be made up only of believers gathering together to form a congregation. This was unlike the Church of England, where people were required to attend the church in their parish, whether they were godly (religious) or not.

▽ William Bradford's Bible traveled to North America with him on the *Mayflower*.

CHURCH ORGANIZATION

For Separatists, the place where they worshipped was of little consequence. In England, the early congregations usually gathered in people's houses. In Plymouth Colony, the settlers' "church" was the bottom floor of the fort, which also doubled as a court and a meeting room. The Separatist church was governed by its members, and its congregations were cared for by "officers" who held the positions of pastor, teacher, elder, deacon, or deaconess. The pastor and teacher were both ordained ministers, responsible for the religious life of their congregations. The elder looked after the day-to-day running of the church, while the deacon and deaconess cared for the sick and poor. Many congregations did not have all of these officers—the Pilgrims, for example, left their pastor behind in Leiden (see page 24). However, we know that John Carver and the colony's doctor, Samuel Fuller, were deacons in the early Plymouth church. It is possible that the deaconess was Samuel's wife, Bridget, who arrived in 1623.

The chart below gives you a general overview of the range of religious beliefs in the early 17th century.

Separatist	Protestant	Roman Catholic
No church organization	Many different church organizations	Single universal (catholic) church organization headed by a pope
Governed by its members	The Church of England retained hierarchical structure headed by bishops	Hierarchical structure headed by a pope
No church building necessary for worship	Plain church buildings, to avoid the worship of idols	Highly decorated churches
Emphasis on individual prayer and belief	Prayer and services laid down in prayer books	Services in Latin, controlled by a priest
Bible translated	Bible translated	Bible in Latin

BUSINESS DEAL

Although the Pilgrim community was based on religious ideals, there was also a commercial (business) aspect to the voyage. In 1617, when the Pilgrims decided to leave Leiden, they sent two of their members with business experience, John Carver and Robert Cushman, to negotiate with the Virginia Company of London. Founded in 1606, this company had already established a settlement at Jamestown, in the region named Virginia by Walter Raleigh in 1585.

The Pilgrims applied to the company for a "patent" (right) to set up a self-governing religious colony in Virginia. In fact, the agreement with the Virginia Company was abandoned when the *Mayflower* made landfall beyond the lands controlled by the company. A new contract was eventually drawn up with the Council of New England, which held a new charter (1620) for the New England territory. The Pilgrims raised money for their venture from **investors** known as the Merchant Adventurers. The Pilgrims were to repay their debts over the first seven years of the colony's existence, partly by sending back goods such as furs to be sold in England. Bradford lists the terms of the contract, agreed upon in 1620, in his journal.

▽ The two sides of the seal of the Virginia Company are shown here. The company was founded by royal charter by King James I, with the purpose of establishing English settlements in North America.

WHO IN HISTORY

ROBERT CUSHMAN   **BORN**: Kent, England
1577/8–1625

ROLE: A member of the Leiden congregation, Cushman's business skills meant that the Pilgrims entrusted much of the organization of the voyage to North America to him. He did not sail on the *Mayflower*, but he arrived in Plymouth Colony in 1621 on the *Fortune*. He became the agent for the colony, buying supplies, selling the furs and wood that the Pilgrims sent back to England, and arranging for the remainder of the Leiden congregation to join the Pilgrims.

Did You Know?

When Cushman returned home on the *Fortune* in 1622, he carried with him Bradford and Winslow's account of life in Plymouth Colony. Published as *Mourt's Relation* (see page 25), it was an important tool to persuade other settlers to **emigrate** and ensure the success of the colony.

PILGRIM TRADES

These are some of the known occupations of the Pilgrims:

Person	Occupation	Other information
Isaac Allerton	Tailor	One of the Leiden congregation
Francis Cooke	Woolcomber	One of the Leiden congregation
Francis Eaton	House carpenter	Came from Bristol, Eng.
Samuel Fuller	Doctor and surgeon	A weaver in Leiden
Stephen Hopkins	Tanner (treating animal hides to make leather)	
William Mullins	Shoemaker	Came from Dorking, Eng.; died in first winter
Degory Priest	Hatmaker	Died during first winter
Thomas Rogers	Luxury cloth merchant	Died during first winter
William White	Woolcomber	Died same day as William Mullins

SAINTS AND STRANGERS

Not all the Pilgrims were from the Leiden community, and not all were Separatists. In order to have enough passengers, some people were recruited in England for the voyage. Pilgrims from the Leiden community were known as "Saints," while those from elsewhere were "Strangers." Some of these Strangers were hired for their skills, to help set up the new colony. The best known of them was Captain Myles Standish.

CAPTAIN MYLES STANDISH (?1584–1656)

Standish was hired by the Separatists to be in charge of the defense of the colony not only against native peoples, but also potential French, Spanish, and Dutch attacks. He had fought in the army of Queen Elizabeth I, and it seems that he became acquainted with the Separatists in Leiden when he was stationed in the Netherlands. He sailed on the *Mayflower* and led the first expeditions to find a suitable site for settlement. Standish was very active in the colony, organizing the construction of the fort and mounting both trading and military expeditions. He also made several voyages back to England to take trading goods on the colonists' behalf. In the 1630s, he established a home in a new town just north of Plymouth, called Duxbury.

▼ This image of Captain Myles Standish standing with an American Indian man is from an illustration to a poem written by Henry Wadsworth Longfellow in 1858.

HISTORY DETECTIVES:
BUILDING UP A PICTURE

Using more than one primary source can help to build up a fuller picture of a person or an event. Sometimes two accounts of the same event can be quite different. The following observations of Captain Standish reveal very different sides to his character.

William Bradford wrote of his gratitude to the six or seven adults who remained healthy during the first terrible winter in the colony, and who were able to tend to the sick and dying Pilgrims. Among these seven were: "Mr. William Brewster, the reverend Elder, and Myles Standish, the Captain and military commander, unto whom my self, and many others, were much beholden in our low and sick condition…"

Another account written in 1680 by a colonist named William Hubbard revealed a rather different characteristic: he described Standish as "a man of very little stature, yet of a very hot and angry temper."

In 1628, Captain Standish arrested Thomas Morton, a colonist who had established a trading settlement called Merrymount, in Massachusetts Bay. The settlers in Plymouth Colony were scandalized by Morton's activities and behavior. This is William Bradford's account: "They… set up a **Maypole**, drinking and dancing about it many days together, inviting the Indian [American Indian] women, for their consorts, dancing and frisking together."

Morton put his own, rather different, side of the story in his book *New English Canaan*. He accused the Pilgrims of being envious of the "prosperity" of Merrymount, and he gave Standish the irreverent nickname "Captain Shrimp."

WHAT HAPPENED TO THEM ON THE JOURNEY?

The Pilgrims actually rented two ships. In July 1620, the *Mayflower* sailed to Southampton from Rotherhithe, in London, to load supplies. Meanwhile another ship called the *Speedwell* brought the Leiden Pilgrims from the Netherlands to Southampton. The plan was for both ships to take them across the Atlantic. After some last-minute negotiations with the investors, the two ships left Southampton for North America on August 5.

Three days later, it became obvious that the *Speedwell* was leaking. By August 10, there was so much water coming into the ship that the pumps could not cope, and the Pilgrims were forced to sail into the nearest safe harbor in England, called Dartmouth. The delay while repairs were carried out on the *Speedwell* was a difficult time for the Pilgrims. Some of the passengers began to have doubts about the whole enterprise. In addition, the food that was meant to last for the voyage and beyond was quickly being used up. The Pilgrims could not afford to waste much more time.

▽ This shows the *Mayflower* and the *Speedwell* in Dartmouth Harbor. This painting is by the 20th-century artist Lesley Arthur Wilcox.

CUSHMAN'S DOUBTS

Robert Cushman (see page 33) was a passenger on the *Speedwell*.
On August 17, 1620, Cushman wrote from Dartmouth to his friend
Edward Southworth about his troubles on the journey:

> My most kind remembrance to you and your wife...whom in this
> world I never look to see again. For besides the eminent dangers of
> this voyage, which are no less than deadly, an infirmity of body hath
> seized me, which will not in all likelihood leave me till death...

> Our pinnace [the Speedwell] will not cease leaking... We put in
> here to trim [repair] her; and I think, as others also, if we had
> stayed at sea but three or four hours more, she would have sunk
> right down... Our victuals [food] will be half eaten up, I think,
> before we go from the coast of England, and if our voyage last
> long, we shall not have a month's victuals when we come in the
> country [North America].

THE *SPEEDWELL* IS ABANDONED

The Pilgrims left England for a second time on August 23. This time, the
ships sailed more than 300 miles (480 kilometers) before being forced to
turn back once again because of leaks in the *Speedwell*. They headed
toward Plymouth Harbor, where the difficult decision was made to abandon
the *Speedwell* and transfer the supplies to the *Mayflower*. There were now
too many passengers, so the Pilgrim leaders selected who should go and
who should be left behind. We can only imagine Robert Cushman's relief at
being able to stay on dry land and return to London!

LATE ARRIVAL

The *Speedwell's* problems explain why the *Mayflower* set off late and
overcrowded on its voyage to North America. The Pilgrims had hoped to
arrive in their new colony in the summer; it would now be much later and
much colder when they made landfall. The ship was also likely to encounter
worse weather than it would have done a few weeks earlier. The *Mayflower*
sailed for the third and final time on September 6, 1620, this time from
Plymouth. The Pilgrims were to be at sea for 66 long days.

North America

Plymouth
Colony

Cape Cod Bay

Atlantic Ocean

Route of the Mayflower

North America

England

Europe

N

England

Plymouth

Dartmouth

Southampton

London

— Mayflower
— Speedwell

▷ This map shows the Pilgrims' long voyage across the Atlantic Ocean. You can also see the routes of the *Mayflower* and the *Speedwell* along the south coast of England.

HISTORY DETECTIVES:
USING PRIMARY SOURCES

William Bradford's account provides us with the only information we have about the voyage of the *Mayflower*. When you look at any primary source, it is useful to have a checklist of questions to ask about it:

- What type of document is it?
- Who wrote or produced it? What do you know about its creator?
- Where and when was it written or produced?
- Why was it written or produced?
- Do you know whom it was written for?
- Is there any obvious bias?
- Are there any other primary sources you can compare it with?

PILGRIMS' LUCK

In his journal, William Bradford devotes just one short chapter to the voyage. From him we know of the storms that dogged the ship, and of the drama of nearly losing John Howland (see page 4). We know, too, that the Pilgrims were able to help when a huge crack appeared in one of the ship's beams. This crack was potentially very serious—and Captain Jones did not know what to do. Some of the sailors wanted to turn back, but others spoke against this because they feared they would not be paid. Luckily, in the cargo was a "great iron screw"—probably part of the equipment transported by the Pilgrims to build houses in the new colony. They were able to use this screw to clamp the splitting beam together. This repair ensured the voyage could continue, and so, as Bradford wrote, "They committed themselves to the will of God, and resolved to proceed."

WHICH LAND?

From maps drawn by earlier explorers such as Captain John Smith, the Pilgrims knew which part of the coastline they were looking for. However, as they came close to the land, they identified Cape Cod, which was to the north of their intended destination in Virginia. They turned southward toward the mouth of the Hudson River, but Bradford records that after about half a day of sailing, they "fell amongst dangerous shoals and roaring breakers, and they were so far entangled therewith as they conceived themselves in great danger." Exhausted and desperate to end their voyage, they decided to head for Cape Cod, even though this was not part of the region controlled by the Virginia Company.

ARRIVAL

Bradford wrote: "Being thus arrived in a good harbour and brought safe to land, they fell upon their knees and blessed the God of heaven, who had brought them over the vast and furious ocean, and delivered them from all the perils and miseries therof." The relief to have completed the perilous voyage is clear in these words. But now the Pilgrims looked fearfully at the unknown land that awaited them. As Bradford put it: "They had now no friends to welcome them, nor inns to entertain or refresh their weatherbeaten bodies, no houses or much less towns to repair to, to seek for succor [help]." It was a daunting prospect. To make matters worse, the crew of the *Mayflower* was eager to dump the Pilgrims and head for home as soon as possible, before the winter storms set in.

THE MAYFLOWER COMPACT

The Pilgrims had landed in New England, outside the boundaries of Virginia. Some of the "Strangers" among the passengers now began to threaten to "use their own liberty" when they went ashore, rather than abiding by any agreement that had been made in England. To avert this crisis, the Pilgrim leaders drew up a document that has become known as the Mayflower Compact. It was an attempt to establish a form of self-government for the new colony until permission could be obtained from the Council of New England for the settlement at Plymouth. Forty-one out of the sixty-five adult male passengers (some of the male servants and hired men did not sign) signed the compact on November 11, 1620. Then they elected John Carver as their first governor.

HISTORY DETECTIVES: HOW DO WE KNOW?

The original Mayflower Compact has been lost. But we know its wording from *Mourt's Relation*, from Bradford's journal, and from a later publication by Bradford's nephew, Nathaniel Morton, called *New England's Memorial* (1669). Morton was the son of George Morton, who organized the publication of *Mourt's Relation*. He came to Plymouth in 1623 and worked as the colony's secretary from 1645. Without his record, we would not know who had signed the compact—unlike Bradford and Winslow, he listed the 41 Pilgrim signers.

▽ This early 20th-century painting by Edward Moran shows the signing of the Mayflower Compact on board the *Mayflower*.

WHAT HAPPENED TO THEM AFTERWARD?

When the Pilgrims set foot in North America, there was already snow on the ground and it was bitterly cold. One of the first tasks was to rebuild a small boat, called a **shallop**, that they had brought with them in pieces on the *Mayflower*. They would use the shallop to try to find the best place for their settlement.

Meanwhile, groups of colonists went ashore to bathe and wash their clothes and to find firewood and drinking water. Without a boat, this was not easy, as the Pilgrims had to wade through the freezing shallows to get to land. Winslow reported that this did not help the Pilgrims' health, as getting wet so frequently, and living in damp clothes, brought on "coughs and colds."

FIRST EXPLORATIONS

While the carpenter was working on the shallop, the Pilgrims decided to mount the first expedition to explore the country. Sixteen men volunteered to go, under the leadership of Captain Myles Standish, to look for native peoples and for a river where they could make their settlement. Although they caught sight of some American Indians, they were unable to make contact with them.

The Pilgrims did, however, come across a deserted American Indian settlement, where they found a kettle from a European ship and large baskets of corn buried beneath the ground. Edward Winslow describes the Pilgrims' dilemma. They desperately needed this food, but would they be stealing if they took it? He wrote:

> At length, after much consultation, we concluded to take the kettle and as much of the corn as we could carry away with us; and when our shallop came, if we could find any of the people, and come to parley [talk] with them, we would give them the kettle again, and satisfy [pay] them for their corn.

HISTORY DETECTIVES:
THE LANDING OF THE PILGRIMS

The only reliable picture we have of any of the Pilgrims is a portrait of Edward Winslow (see page 25). All other paintings showing scenes from the Pilgrims' lives are imaginative. One of the most celebrated is by the American artist Henry Sargent (1770–1845), showing the moment the Pilgrims first stepped on North American soil. In this huge painting, the two central figures are Samoset and Governor John Carver (center). Of course, we know from historical records that Samoset did not walk into the Pilgrims' lives until March 1621 (see page 46). But for the artist, the presence of Samoset as the Pilgrims step on shore adds drama to this already dramatic moment.

THE RIGHT SPOT

Many weeks passed before the Pilgrims were able to decide on the right place to establish their settlement. During this time, many of the Pilgrims were becoming considerably weaker due to poor diet, the extreme cold, and the cramped, unhygienic conditions on the ship. It was clear that they could not last much longer in this state, yet some of them were unwilling to settle down until they were certain they had found a good location. But as Pilgrims began to die in December, the need to move to shore became increasingly urgent. On December 11, 1620, they finally found a place with good anchorage, freshwater streams, and fertile soil. Bradford wrote that "it was the best they could find, and the season, and their present necessity, made them glad to accept of it." By this time, seven of the Pilgrims were already dead.

HISTORY DETECTIVES:
SEARCHING THE INTERNET

Type "Mayflower" into a search engine and you will get a mixture of restaurants, hotels, and florists, plus many web sites about the Pilgrim's ship. Try *"Mayflower Pilgrims"* or *"Mayflower ship"* and the search narrows. One of the best sites for Mayflower research is Caleb Johnson's MayflowerHistory.com. Johnson has written several books about the *Mayflower* and its passengers, and his web site is a mine of useful information, as well as primary sources. You can find lots of other useful web sites on pages 62–63.

Work on constructing the first houses in Plymouth Colony began. The Pilgrims had to chop down trees and split logs to make planks for houses. It was tough work in awful conditions—they were dogged by the rain and cold, and when gales blew up they had no choice but to retreat to the *Mayflower*. The deaths continued throughout the bitter month of January.

△ This is a reconstruction of Plymouth Colony, looking toward Cape Cod Bay.

WHAT WAS KILLING THE PILGRIMS?

Bradford recorded the terrible death toll of the first winter in Plymouth:

> But that which was most sad and lamentable was, that in 2 or 3 months time half of their company died, especially in Jan[uary] and February, being the depth of winter, and wanting houses and other comforts; being infected with the **scurvy** and other diseases...so as there died some times 2 or 3 of a day, in the foresaid time; that of 100 and odd persons, scarce 50 remained...

We don't know exactly what disease was killing the Pilgrims, but it was probably a combination of scurvy from their inadequate diet, mentioned by Bradford, and the "coughs and colds" (pneumonia) noted by Winslow.

MEETINGS WITH AMERICAN INDIANS

When the Pilgrims decided to emigrate to North America, they knew that they would have to live alongside the native peoples of this unknown land. From the outset, they were eager to establish friendly relations with the local American Indians and were fearful of attack. Their first encounter was a hostile one. In early December 1620, a party of Pilgrims out looking for a settlement site were attacked by about 40 American Indians. The Pilgrims defended themselves, and no one was killed or injured.

Although the Pilgrims remained aware of American Indians from fleeting glimpses, noises, and the occasional smoke from fires, they did not make contact until March 1621. It was then that an American Indian walked straight into the Pilgrims' new settlement and welcomed them in broken English. His name was Samoset, and he had learned some English from colonists in his home region of Maine. He told them that he knew another American Indian, Tisquantum (Squanto), who spoke even better English because he had traveled to England. The Pilgrims were both amazed and fascinated.

THE WAMPANOAG

The Pilgrims found out from Samoset that the spot where they had chosen to build their settlement had until recently been home to the Patuxet. Samoset told them that a terrible plague had killed off all the Patuxet a few years earlier. Historians now think that this "plague" may have been a type of **hepatitis**, brought by European settlers and spread through contaminated food.

From Samoset, the Pilgrims also learned that it was the Nauset who had attacked them in December. According to Samoset, the Nauset were incensed by the behavior of the English captain, Thomas Hunt (see page 47), who had kidnapped several of their people to sell them as slaves. Both the Nauset and the Patuxet were part of a confederation (larger group) called the Wampanoag ("easterners"), who lived in southeastern Massachusetts. Samoset stayed with the Pilgrims overnight, and the next day they presented him with a knife, bracelet, and ring. As he left, he promised to return soon with some of their American Indian neighbors.

TISQUANTUM (also known as SQUANTO) ?–1622
BORN: Probably in Patuxet (Plymouth, Massachusetts)

ROLE: Tisquantum helped the Pilgrims to survive their first year in Plymouth. We know nothing about his early life until 1614, when European ships arrived at Cape Cod. One of the lieutenants, Thomas Hunt, persuaded several Nauset and Patuxet to come aboard his ship. He then kidnapped them, taking them to Spain, where he hoped to sell them as slaves. Not surprisingly, this treatment outraged the Wampanoag, who became extremely hostile to European arrivals. Tisquantum, however, managed to find his way to England, where he worked for the Newfoundland Company. On a trip to Newfoundland, he met Thomas Dermer, who was employed by the New England Company. Dermer recognized that Tisquantum, who now spoke good English, would be a useful go-between to try to make peace with the Nauset and Patuxet. In 1619, Dermer and Tisquantum returned to Cape Cod. They found that Tisquantum's village was now a deserted burial ground, with all of its inhabitants dead.

Did You Know?

In 1622, Tisquantum began bleeding from the nose. He told the Pilgrims that this was a sign he would soon die, which was proven true. Bradford wrote, "His death was a great loss."

MASSASOIT

A few days after his first visit, Samoset brought Tisquantum to meet the Pilgrims. Tisquantum offered to introduce them to Massasoit, the sachem (leader) of the Wampanoag. On March 22, 1621, the Pilgrims and Massasoit drew up a treaty. Both Bradford and Winslow report the terms of this agreement. Bradford, who was still writing his journal many years later, also tells us that the treaty proved to be long-lasting.

PEACE TREATY

From *Mourt's Relation*:

1. That neither he [Massasoit] nor any of his should injure or do hurt to any of our people.
2. And if any of his did hurt to any of ours, he should send the offender, that we might punish him.
3. That if any of our tools were taken away when our people are at work, he should cause them to be restored, and if ours did any harm to any of his, we would do the likewise to them.
4. If any did unjustly war against him, we would aid him; if any did war against us, he should aid us.
5. He should send to his neighbour confederates, to certify them of this, that they might not wrong us, but might be likewise comprised [included] in the conditions of peace.
6. That when their men came to us, they should leave their bows and arrows behind them, as we should do our pieces [guns] when we came to them.

WHY?

Many historians have asked why Massasoit allowed the Pilgrims to settle in Plymouth and why he drew up a peace treaty with them. The answer lies in the terrible plague that had killed the inhabitants of Tisquantum's village and many thousands more of the Wampanoag. It is thought that the disease killed off 90 percent of the American Indians in coastal New England. This left the region empty and open for settlement by Europeans—as the

⚠ Massasoit, leader of the Wampanoag, signs the earliest recorded treaty in New England, with Governor John Carver in 1621.

Pilgrims had found. It also left the Wampanoag significantly weakened, particularly in relation to the hostile Narragansett—the confederation of people who lived to the west in present-day Rhode Island. Massasoit calculated that making peace with the Europeans would be helpful protection against the Narragansett.

MODEL PILGRIMS?

Pictures and descriptions of the Pilgrims often give the rather romantic impression that they were all model colonists. But some of them were definitely sinners rather than "Saints." John Billington boarded the *Mayflower* with his wife and two children. It was the younger boy, Francis, who nearly blew up the *Mayflower*, just after the Pilgrims arrived off Cape Cod, by playing with his father's musket (gun) on the ship. And as soon as the *Mayflower* left, John began to question the command of Captain Standish and the Pilgrim leaders. John Billington continued to cause trouble in the colony and was eventually hanged for murder in 1630.

ON THEIR OWN

At the beginning of April 1621, the *Mayflower* finally left the colony to sail back to England. None of the Pilgrims chose to return. After the departure of the *Mayflower*, Bradford describes how the Pilgrims busied themselves with building up their food supplies. They received considerable help from Tisquantum, who showed them how to plant their corn, how to catch fish, and how to set traps. His knowledge was invaluable, and without him, it is unlikely the colony would have survived that first year.

However, tragedy continued to strike with the sudden death of the colony's first governor, John Carver, probably from sunstroke. Nevertheless, the Pilgrims who survived had a summer of plentiful food—good crops, plenty of fish, birds, and other meat, including turkey and venison (meat from deer). At some point around late September or early October, the Pilgrims gave thanks for this harvest with a feast, held with Massasoit and their American Indian neighbors.

▼ This is an artist's interpretation of the return of the *Mayflower* to England, as it left the Pilgrims behind to fend for themselves in their new colony.

Think About This

Departure of the Mayflower

The moment when the *Mayflower* finally left must have been an emotional one for the colonists. They were now on their own, with no way of knowing how or when they would have contact with their loved ones back in Europe. What would you have chosen to do? Stay to face the unknown in North America, or return to an uncertain future in England or the Netherlands?

THE *FORTUNE*

On November 9, 1621, the Pilgrims saw a sailing ship appear over the horizon. This was the *Fortune*, set out from England to sail direct to Plymouth. It carried Robert Cushman and 35 others who wished to remain in the colony. However, the excitement of greeting these new settlers was dampened by the realization that they brought with them virtually no supplies or equipment! Suddenly, the Pilgrims' food supplies, carefully laid in for the winter, looked less abundant for a colony of more than 80 people. Bradford remarked in his journal: "The plantation [colony] was glad of this addition of strength, but could have wished that many of them had been of better condition, and all of them better furnished with provisions; but that could not now be helped."

Cushman also brought unwelcome news from the investors back in London, who were angry that the *Mayflower* had returned carrying only a few trading goods. Bradford wrote a letter to the investors, explaining the sorry tale of the colonists' first winter. The *Fortune* did not stay long in Plymouth. The ship set sail again within two weeks, carrying Robert Cushman and as many goods as the Pilgrims could manage, including "clapboard" (pieces of timber) and beaver and otter skins provided by Tisquantum.

WHY WAS THEIR JOURNEY SIGNIFICANT?

The Pilgrims survived their second winter at Plymouth Plantation, despite having extra mouths to feed. By 1623, most of the original community from Leiden had made the journey to join their families. Publications such as *Mourt's Relation* and *Good News from New England* encouraged more settlers to come to this "Promised Land." By the 1630s, there were many Puritan settlements being established in the Massachusetts Bay area.

THE PILGRIM STORY

The Pilgrims were not the first European settlers in North America. So, why have they captured the imagination of successive generations? The traditional elements of the Pilgrims' story include the flight from persecution, the voyage and struggle for survival, and Thanksgiving. But as we have seen, their history is far more complex.

▼ This map shows the locations of American Indian tribes as well as the Puritan settlements.

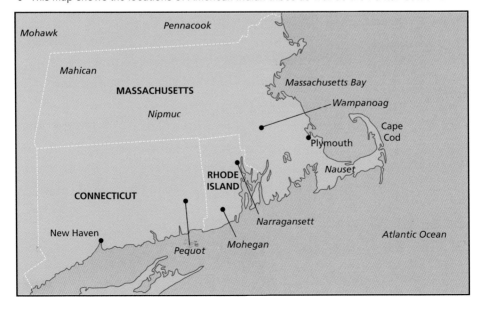

To start with, the Pilgrims had found religious freedom in the Netherlands, so rather than fleeing immediate persecution, the reasons for their decision to leave were more varied. And we know that many of the people on board the *Mayflower* were not Separatists at all, but rather were passengers recruited to help the colony pay its way. The Pilgrims barely survived the first winter and, once spring arrived, they probably owed their subsequent survival to an American Indian, Tisquantum. As for Thanksgiving, the true origins of this annual holiday are examined on pages 54 and 55.

LAYING THE FOUNDATIONS

Like other settlers from England, the Pilgrims set up their colony as a commercial venture in order to raise the funds to go to North America. But what was different about the Pilgrims, despite the mix of "Saints" and "Strangers" on the *Mayflower*, was their shared religious faith and the social contract expressed in the Mayflower Compact. The original Mayflower Compact may be long lost, but the ideas it documented laid the foundation for future democratic government in the United States.

PLYMOUTH ROCK

On the waterfront in modern-day Plymouth, Massachusetts, lies the "Plymouth Rock." According to tradition, this rock marks the landing point of the Pilgrims in 1620. However, Bradford and Winslow do not mention such a rock. In fact, the story only really surfaced around 120 years after the Pilgrims made landfall, when a local man told the story of the rock. It is an example of "oral tradition"—a story that has been passed down by word of mouth over generations and has been changed along the way. Despite this, the Plymouth Rock remains a powerful reminder of the Pilgrims.

THANKSGIVING

Every year on the fourth Thursday in November, Americans celebrate the festival of Thanksgiving. It is true that the origins of this festival go back to the harvest feast held by the Pilgrims with Massasoit and the Wampanoag in 1621. But what many people do not realize is that the Pilgrims never called this "thanksgiving," and that there is little mention of it in the primary sources from the period (see the box on page 55). Nor did the Pilgrims hold a regular "thanksgiving" celebration. It was only after 1863, when President Abraham Lincoln declared it a national holiday, that Thanksgiving became an annual event across the United States.

THANKSGIVING MENU

The modern-day Thanksgiving meal centers on turkey with stuffing, cranberry sauce, potatoes, and pumpkin pie. It is Bradford who mentions "wild turkey," and we know that the Pilgrims also caught and ate many other types of fowl, including duck, geese, swan, and even eagles. It is possible that the Pilgrims stuffed their birds with herbs or onions, or possibly oats. But it is unlikely that they enjoyed cranberry sauce with their meat—sugar was an expensive item in the 17th century, and it is unlikely the Pilgrims had a supply of it at this point. They may have had pumpkins and squashes, which grew in that region, but it is unlikely that they had flour and fat to make crust for a pie.

▽ This romantic view of the "first Thanksgiving" in 1621 is taken from a painting by American artist J. L. G. Ferris.

HISTORY DETECTIVES:
EVIDENCE FOR THANKSGIVING

There are two primary sources that give us information about the Pilgrims' harvest in 1621. In a letter printed at the end of *Mourt's Relation*, Edward Winslow describes the feast. William Bradford, writing in his journal, does not mention a feast specifically, but he does include a reference to turkeys.

Winslow wrote:

> Our harvest being gotten in, our governor sent four men on fowling, that so we might after a special manner rejoice together after we had gathered the fruit of our labors… At which time…many of the Indians coming amongst us, and among the rest their greatest king Massasoit, with some ninety men, whom for three days we entertained and feasted, and they went out and killed five deer, which they brought to the plantation and bestowed on our governor, and upon the captain and others. And although it be not always so plentiful as it was at this time with us, yet by the goodness of God, we are so far from want that we often wish you partakers of our plenty.

Bradford wrote:

> All the summer there was no want; and now began to come in store of fowl, as winter approached, of which this place did abound when they came first (but afterward decreased by degrees). And besides waterfowl there was great store of wild turkeys, of which they took many, besides venison, etc.

FOUNDING FATHERS

For many people, the Pilgrim story is the story of the founding of the modern-day United States. The saga of bravery, faith, and perseverance shown by the Pilgrims continues to inspire today. The fact that they did make a success of Plymouth Colony—with a great deal of help from the local American Indians—encouraged others to follow their example.

PURITAN SETTLEMENTS

In England, Puritans continued to experience persecution and harassment. In 1628, a group of Puritan merchants gained permission to found a colony in the Massachusetts Bay area, north of Plymouth. Between 1630 and 1640, thousands of Puritans migrated to Massachusetts. The first governor of the Massachusetts Bay Colony, John Winthrop, arrived on the *Arbella* in 1630.

PEQUOT WAR

The arrival of so many new settlers inevitably caused problems with the local American Indians. The first major conflict that involved both the Plymouth colonists and the more recent Massachusetts Bay settlers was the Pequot War of 1637–1638. The Pequots lived in the Connecticut River valley, but their territory was threatened by the expansion of the Puritan

▼ This 19th-century image shows the massacre of the Pequot by English settlers in Massachusetts Bay.

colonies. The Narragansett and Mohegans helped the English settlers to defeat the Pequot. The destruction of the Pequot was ruthless, as Bradford noted in his journal: "Those that escaped the fire were slain with the sword; some hewed to pieces, others run throw [through] with their rapiers [swords], so as they were quickly dispatched, and very few escaped."

BEGINNINGS AND ENDS

In 1643, Plymouth became part of the New England Confederation, together with the Puritan colonies of Massachusetts, Connecticut, and New Haven. This was the first attempt to create a union between the independent colonies. In the following year, William Bradford sadly recorded the death of Elder Brewster. At the same time, he marveled that so many of the Pilgrims who survived the difficult first months of their time in Plymouth had gone on to live to ripe old ages (at a time when life expectancy was much lower than today), saying:

I cannot but here take occasion, not only to mention, but greatly to admire the marvelous providence of God, that notwithstanding the many changes and hardships that these people went through, and the many enemies they had and difficulties they met with all, that so many of them should live to very old age!

Bradford himself died in 1657, at the age of 67.

MAYFLOWER DESCENDANTS

Millions of people can claim to be descended from the *Mayflower* Pilgrims. They have included some famous names:

- Bing Crosby (singer—descended from William Brewster)
- Marilyn Monroe (actor—descended from John Alden and William Mullins)
- Christopher Reeve (actor—descended from William Bradford)
- Alan B. Shepard (Moon astronaut—descended from Richard Warren).

You can find out more about *Mayflower* descendants at:

www.sail1620. org/history/ notable-mayflower-descendants/90-notable-descendants.html.

TIMELINE

1606	Start date of William Bradford's journal
1607	The first attempt of Scrooby Separatists to leave England fails
1607	Founding of Jamestown, Virginia
1608	Scrooby Separatists escape England for the Netherlands
1609	Scrooby Separatists settle in Leiden, in the Netherlands
1616	Publication of *A Description of New England* by Captain John Smith
1617	Separatists decide to leave Leiden; they begin negotiations with the Virginia Company
1620	***July 22***: *Speedwell* leaves the Netherlands ***July 26***: *Mayflower* and *Speedwell* meet in Southampton, England ***Aug. 5***: *Mayflower* and *Speedwell* set off from Southampton ***Aug. 10***: *Mayflower* and *Speedwell* change course for Dartmouth, England, to repair leaks in the *Speedwell* ***Aug. 23***: *Mayflower* and *Speedwell* leave Dartmouth ***Aug. 28***: Both ships return to Plymouth, in England, because of leaks in the *Speedwell* ***Sept. 6***: *Mayflower* sets off from Plymouth with 102 Pilgrims on board for a 66-day voyage ***Nov. 11***: Arrival off the coast of Cape Cod, in North America; signing of the Mayflower Compact ***Dec. 8***: Pilgrims have first skirmish with American Indians ***Dec. 11***: Pilgrims decide on a settlement spot (remembered as "Forefathers' Day")

1621	**Jan.–Feb.**: Many Pilgrims die due to malnutrition, cold, and associated illnesses
	March 16: Samoset arrives in the Pilgrims' settlement
	March 21: Treaty agreed to between the Pilgrims and Massasoit
	April 5: *Mayflower* leaves the Pilgrims to sail back to England
	Late Sept./early Oct.: Pilgrims celebrate the harvest with Massasoit and the Wampanoag
	Nov. 9: Arrival of the *Fortune*
1622	Publication of *A Relation or Journal…of the English Plantation Settled at Plymouth* (*Mourt's Relation*)
	Nov.: Tisquantum dies
1623	Two more ships, *Anne* and *Little James,* arrive in Plymouth
1624	Last official record of the *Mayflower;* by this time, there are around 180 people living in Plymouth Colony
1625	Reverend John Robinson dies in Leiden
1630	John Winthrop, first governor of Massachusetts Bay Colony, arrives on the *Arbella*
1630–1640	Thousands of Puritans settle the Massachusetts Bay area
1637–1638	Pequot War
1643	Plymouth becomes part of the New England Confederation
1644	Death of Elder William Brewster
1657	Death of William Bradford

GLOSSARY

archive collection of historical records, usually primary source documents

barber-surgeon dating from medieval times in Europe, before surgery was a separate profession, barber-surgeons performed procedures such as bloodletting and pulling out teeth

bias having an unfair or unbalanced opinion

canvas heavy, strong, plain fabric that is made from hemp, cotton, or linen. Traditionally, it was used for making sails as well as tents. It is also used by artists as a surface to paint on.

colonist person who lives in a settlement called a colony

colony settlement made by emigrants in a territory far from their home country, which keeps ties with the parent country

elder in the Separatist church of the Pilgrims, the elder was one of the church officers who was responsible for the management of the congregation

emigrate leave one's home country to settle permanently in another country

hepatitis medical condition caused by inflammation of the liver

hierarchical any system of persons or things that are ranked one above another

investor someone who invests money in a business or a project in the expectation of making the money back plus a profit at some point in the future

lawsuit claim or dispute that goes to court in order to decide a fair resolution

maritime relating to the sea

master in the 17th century, the master of a ship was the captain

maypole tall wooden pole used in many European folk celebrations, but particularly for May Day. People often danced around the maypole.

native people original inhabitants of a particular country or region

ordain make someone a priest or minister

pilot in a ship, the person responsible for navigation, particularly when the ship is close to land

Protestant term used to describe any of the churches that emerged during the Reformation of the 16th century, which rejected the universal authority of the pope and the Roman Catholic Church. The term comes from the Latin for "one who protests."

Puritan group of English Protestants in the 16th and 17th centuries, who got their names because they insisted on "purity" of belief and practice. They believed that the Church of England retained too many practices from the Catholic Church and wanted more reforms.

rigging ropes and chains that support the masts on a ship. They are used to control the sails.

Roman Catholic Church Christian church that is based in the Vatican in Rome, Italy, with the pope at its head

scurvy disease caused by a lack of vitamin C. It was once common among sailors who were at sea for a long time, because it was difficult to store fresh fruits and vegetables, the main source of this vitamin.

Separatist in the 16th and 17th centuries, any of the groups of reformers in England who wanted to split entirely from the Church of England and set up their own independent local churches

shallop small open boat fitted with oars and sails for use mainly in shallow, coastal waters

FIND OUT MORE

BOOKS

Arenstam, Peter. *Mayflower 1620: A New Look at a Pilgrim Voyage*. Washington, D.C.: National Geographic Society, 2007.

Philbrick, Nathaniel. *The Mayflower and the Pilgrims' New World*. New York: G. P. Putnam's Sons, 2008.

WEB SITES

www.histarch.uiuc.edu/plymouth/index2.html

mith.umd.edu//eada

You can find primary sources on both these web sites.

mayflowerhistory.com

Caleb Johnson's web site is a treasure trove of information about the *Mayflower* and the Pilgrims, and it includes a broad selection of useful primary sources.

memory.loc.gov/ammem/collections/jefferson_papers/mtjvatm.html

You can find out more about the Virginia Company and the history of early settlement in North America on this web site.

www.pilgrimarchives.nl

Visit the Pilgrim Archives web site.

www.pilgrimhallmuseum.org

The web site for the Pilgrim Hall Museum has huge amounts of information about the Pilgrims, all aspects of their story, and about Thanksgiving.

www.plimoth.org

Find out more about the *Mayflower II* and Plymouth Colony at this web site.

www.sail1620.org

Sail 1620 is a web site dedicated to *Mayflower* descendants in Pennsylvania. It also has lots of other useful information.

MUSEUMS

Pilgrim Hall Museum
75 Court Street
Plymouth, Massachusetts 02360
www.pilgrimhallmuseum.org

Pilgrim Monument and Provincetown Museum
High Pole Hill Road
Provincetown, Massachusetts 02657
www.pilgrim-monument.org

Plimoth Plantation
137 Warren Avenue
Plymouth, Massachusetts 02360
www.plimoth.org

OTHER TOPICS TO RESEARCH

There are many interesting topics related to the *Mayflower*. Start with the suggestions below and discover which area holds the most interest for you.

Settlements:
Find out more about the other settlements that existed in North America at the time of the *Mayflower* voyage, such as the one at Jamestown. When was it founded, who founded it, and how did the colonists survive their voyage and first year?

Later voyages:
Find out more about the settlers who arrived in Plymouth after the *Mayflower*. Who sailed on the *Fortune*, the *Anne*, and the *Little James*? How did their arrival affect life in the new colony?

INDEX